WHITE LINEN REMEMBERED

OTHER BOOKS BY MARYA FIAMENGO

The Quality of Halves, Klanak Press (1958)

Overheard at the Oracle, Very Stone Press (1969)

Silt of Iron, Ingluvin Press (1971)

In Praise of Old Women, Mosaic Press (1976)
Second Printing (1977)

North of the Cold Star (New and Selected Poems),
Mosaic Press (1978)

Patience After Compline, Mosaic Press (1989)

White Linen Remembered

POEMS

Marya Fiamengo

RONSDALE
1996

WHITE LINEN REMEMBERED
Copyright © 1996 Marya Fiamengo

RONSDALE PRESS
3350 West 21st Avenue
Vancouver, B.C., Canada
V6S 1G7

Set in Baskerville, 11 pt on 13½
Typesetting: The Typeworks, Vancouver, B.C.
Printing: Hignell Printing, Winnipeg, Manitoba
Cover Design: Cecilia Jang
Cover Art: Joe Plaskett, "Morning: The Open Door"
Author Photo: Marya Fiamengo with the artist Joe Plaskett

The publisher wishes to thank the Canada Council and the British Columbia Cultural Services Branch for their financial assistance.

CANADIAN CATALOGUING IN PUBLICATION DATA

Fiamengo, Marya.
  White linen remembered

Poems.
  ISBN 0-921870-41-8

  1. Title.
PS8511.I2W54   1996   C811'.54   C96-910257-7
PR9199.3.F515W54   1996

This book is dedicated to

Joseph Plaskett
for his inspired art

and

Russell Thornton
with gratitude
for his assistance with my work

ACKNOWLEDGEMENTS

Thanks to the editors of the following magazines and anthologies where some of the poems in this book were first published:

"White Linen Remembered" in *Words We Call Home*, Editor, Linda Svendsen

"On Paragons, Animals and Wild Birds" in *Because You Loved Being a Stranger*, Editor, Susan Musgrave

"Hobotniča" in *The Poem Factory*

"At Englishman's River" in *Prism International*

"A Mandala of Birds and Feathers" in *Inside the Poem*, Editor, W.H. New

CONTENTS

I

II

III

IV

V

VI

VII

I

HEALING OBLIVION

*for Dorothy Fraser who made it possible
and Kathleen Brown who was there*

The air of evening resonant
with cedar innocence.

The sky cobalt blue in the light
of the prodigal spendthrift sun.

The wind moves in the rowan trees
red berries bob in the beaks

of omnivorous vital birds. Seraphic
they flutter in a flicker of bright wings.

I plant trees to connect flesh
to fact, release grief

offer foliage for scent. Arbours
for the hum of ambrosial bees.

Plead with the burnished summer
for reprieve from mutability.

Time passes and night assembles
a progeny of stars. I fumble

towards dawn to retrieve
the vivid vivacious dead.

Memoir is the bloom: memory
blossom is the remembering.

Lost orchard at Kilpoola. Vandals
burn the Lacey homestead.

High July heat. A horned owl
dim in the acacia grove.

We pause in the pine trees
sentient with mourning doves.

Stone still meadows. Fragrant Osoyoos
in a haze of amber distance.

The hills catch at the rapport
the clutch of living near water.

The Haynes cattle vanish into
a stain of perfect air.

Rare felicity. Yellow-headed blackbirds
twitter as the dark girl stitches ancestral
                needlework.

Pregnant she sits at ancient patterns
by the aspen tree dreaming

of open country. Vistas lucid
with green luminous grasses.

Her needle a compass point
accepts the truth of promise.

Knows the flow of the river
moves towards healing

dissolves the drought of oblivion.

CRANBERRY FLATS

for Donald Stephens
of Yorkton, Saskatchewan
and
Patrick Lane and Lorna Crozier
who took me
where the river eddies

"The wind blows high, the
wind blows low,"
While children skip
to measure.

I
And in persistent twists
of fate and weather
the wind, it bloweth
as it listeth.

Sunday morning, I
drive through the hurried
sea-stained streets
of a cedar green and grey
seldom golden city
to sit on the blunt wood
of an Anglican pew.

Joined with them
in the fellowship
of worship, I gaze
at the calm white
buttons bright on the shoulders
of the Salish people.

We bend in the reveries
of devotion, breathe
to the fragrance
of incense.

5

And I, lost
in the gentle glitter
of the beaded blankets
slip out of time
and the focus of place.

II

A scent of grass
the lisp of water
my eyes open
on dry dust
redolent of summer.

A horned lark skitters
into a bloom of bushes
the rattle of poplars
twitch of aspen
mixes with plain song.

Cranberry Flats
above the slow sunstruck
flow of the circuitous Saskatchewan
glint in the maze
of an altered mind.

III

Memorial patterns
of prayer continue.
All that is tender
gone, transmuted
into dust motes
nunc dimittis
motets of the infinite
lux perpetua finalized.

Browning's bishop
darts into memory
gnawed by the twin
worms of avarice
and insistent mortality.

Venial in the intrepid
love of porphyry, the lapis
lazuli hues of luxury.
Redeemed from the bias
of matter by the "blessed
mutter of the mass."

IV

Cranberry Flats,
endangered flora,
Salish people,
endangered fauna.
Above the wide
skeletal unassuming sky
augurs eternity.

Outside, dock side,
the salmon fleet moves north.
We wait for the blessing
of loaves and fishes.

The wind sighs
in its drift through Cranberry
thickets shaping the numinous
sound of canticle
praise for sacred places.

NIKOLAI KONSTANTINE
ON THE BEACH

Buoyant amid the changes
     and the chances
     on the rock rough shore
insouciant and unaware
     pale gold in the spring day
     lightly blithe as immortality
Nikolai Konstantine slides
     impulsive feet
     into the shallows
       of the stream.

A woman sits
     her back propped
     by the adamantine strength
     of sea scoured cliffs.

She watches
     eyes attentive
     fixed on the child
as he tumbles and twists
     a pebble tossed
     velocity in the bed
       of the creek.

She considers
     nomenclature its parameters
     kinship its circumference
     of peril.
Russian princes savage
     with autocracy
     power dark they dress
     pain in Byzantine black
       and red.

More remote
    a Roman emperor
    converts to a visionary
    impulse in the sky.

The indifferent titular deity
    of the place
    a somnolent heron
    flaps a grey muffle
of wings towards the distance,
    "where all things wise
    and fair descend."

As Nikolai descends
    the path
    of the creek
directed to the marble sea.

In hoc signo vincet.

The companionable sky
    has not a sign no bars
    of consequential light.

The luminous child
    on the beach
    oblivious to easeful
    death complacent
under the shifting stars
    asks for no defence
    but constancy.

The world behind
    where the traffic
    seethes along the tarmac
        darkling
offers a lesson in uncertainty
        fitful peace.

But he caught by
        the singing of the sea
        glows and glitters
        at the edge
breathes in the crystal
        of reprieve for
        the day's felicity
welcomes tomorrow's possible
            grace.

II

VINKA
    or
The Fabric of Legend

Gentle reader this tale
        improbable as it may
        read is true.

In a hot implacable August
        on a small island
        in a smaller village
        these events occurred.

At dawn my uncle
        wakes me to the sight
        and sound of the sea
        seraphic on the nearby shore.

Gently I am placed
        on his household vehicle
        a patient elderly donkey.

Today is the day we visit
        Great Aunt Vinka in the hills
        beyond Great St. Nikola.

We climb steeply
        into those hills filled
        with the scent of heaven
        wild thyme redolent rosemary.

Below us the Adriatic
        preens in the morning air
        by the wayside lemon trees
        compete with wild oak

Each soothed by
    the constant syllabic hum
    of mourning doves the startled
    slither of hares in the limestone outcrop.

The path leads
    to a clearing where wild olives
    back against a stone ascent
    of clambering cliff.

Sovereign in the door
    of a dim oracular cave
    dressed in black so worn
    it shines grey white

Tall and gaunt
    as her gnarled olive grove
    spindle in her hand
    stands my great aunt, Vinka.

A woman grown
    not old but ancient
    as temple ruins and crumpled
    city walls are ancient.

Matriarchal she bends
    to bless me looks direct
    unequivocal into my startled
    eyes. She nods recognition.

The air stunned
    into silence by the heat
    of noon is punctured by
    the rasp of cicadas.

And our formal halting greetings.

She looms before us
        the village sybil, healer
        and seer, the clairvoyant
        voice of augury.

Before speaking she smiles
        her mouth free of teeth
        is generous with portent
        the power of utterance.

Her voice is silver
        a silver thread in a fabled
        morning as the spindle she holds
        is mythic with the power
        to weave legend.

We give her honey
        bread with goat's cheese
        a dark harsh wine
        red grapes, black olives.

I part with her reluctant
        leaving behind devoted
        a particle of memory
        enshrined forever votive
        in my future mind.

As we leave
        she calls after me, "Little niece
        comfort yourself with singing
        for you will not be happy
        until late in life."

We move downward
        the sardonic Adriatic sun
        beats a bruise of heat
        into our shelterless backs.

All this was in another country.

I comfort myself with singing.

WHITE LINEN REMEMBERED

"Tamo daleko ..."

I

CODES TO EXISTENCE

If all manner of things
are to be well,
are to be well remembered,
as flowers are codes, birds
alphabets to existence

then childhood
is white linen. White linen
cross-stitched with crimson. With
petals. Flowers abstracted.

Gardens are roses. Carnations
and camomile. Rosemary.
The grass sprinkled with thyme.
Border fragrance. Lavender.
The scent fond. Remembering.

Soft speech. Strangers
framed in doorways.
The custom of courtesy.
Wine served. The best.
In the Sunday glass.

My father present
in absence. Counterpoint
of names which nourish
the folklore of fishing,
fables of origin. Namu.
Mostar. Rivers Inlet.
Vis. Seymour Narrows.
Sarajevo. Hecate Strait.

Hecate, goddess
of crossings. Shadows.
We left behind in an
abandoned convent. Haunted
by ghosts of misplaced nuns.

Friends come. In the early
grace of the day's time. Large
corded men. Civil with
laughter. Welcome the dower
white linen of olive dark
women.

Sunlight on stone. Leeside
we shelter. Catch at confidences.
The harbour at Hvar. Olive
and lemon grove. Tapestry
of shared affection. Komiža.
Ancestral fig tree. Prophetic
Nis. Skull tower. Ohrid.
Angelic fresco.

II

THE LIME TREE

I pause. Bemused by traffic.
On a prosperous thoroughfare. Stand
in a shop. Listen to the simmer
of shoppers. Shopkeeper's talk.

Hear the familiar: the language.
Dialect maternal
accent paternal
content inimical.

Unwilling the ear records
faction. Small mean
hate. Malice of region

18

erupts in the spittle of failed
fascists. Love of commerce
not kindred. The remaining
rancid rampart of the blessed:
the Croatian bourgeoisie.

Hint of contempt
in the price of purchase
black grapes green olives.
Homage to Dalmatia
not Ustasha madness.

Accidental as pleasure. A lime
tree planted. Grown for fidelity.
Love of the allusive. Fitful
years later. Learn it sacred.
Sacred in Serbia.

Expansive with summer
the leaves fill the garden
face the salt
of the sea. Acknowledge
Eastern approaches to history.
The hard red star. Resistance.

The silt of iron settles
in the mouth of the river.
Olive dark the women,
ceremony of stitches
finished. Wither.

My father vatic traverses
the straights of narrowed
passage. My mother
elemental dissolves
into sea mist. The red
star rides on the tide
elegiac.

19

HOBOTNIČA
(The Octopus)

                    I
The old ghosts
              mourn.
The young cry
              out
their grief. Bitter
harvest at the end
of summer. Apples
of discord chewed
by black teeth.

I recall
my mother
leaning
on a withered
wooden fence.
Her kerchief
like the fabric
of her country
                  torn.

She speaks
of her youth.
How as a very
young girl, a child
                  almost
she walked
to the sea
at the end
of her garden.

Walked to where
in the clear
water swam
the octopus, the innocent
                  hobotniča.

She dips
a dazzle
of white linen
into the pristine blue
        of the Adriatic
making a blaze
of whiteness
enticing the pink
        and white
sea creature
into its milky
        folds.

Artless
he swims
into the crystal
cream of its weave.

Triumphant
she holds him
        fast.
Ties a swift
        knot.
Takes him home
for the family
        evening meal.

II

Later
much later
she moves to a distant
        harbour.
Rests the weight
of her pain
on clinical linen.

One dawn
a grave celebrant
expected, solicitous
lays on the lap
of her years
a length of bleached
              cloth
enticing this pink
              and grey
land creature
into the blanched small bones
of his stone embrace.

          White
on blue I shroud
her in my father's
colours. In the green
of grape leaves, the purple
pall of vineyards. Gold
for the light on the Adriatic.

          Adieu
to both. Last stars
lost stars. I hear
you in the hour
of vespers. See
you move past
the thuggish dissonance
of present history
into the bold eye
of the clear
              morning.

THE PEAR TREE

Summer is stitching. Sewing
red thread into a circular
dazzle of cloth. Red stitches
        on white linen.

You ask to walk. Toward
the pear tree whose white
petals thick in the luminous
dark of a late spring
break on the eye like
        a froth on milk.

You are heavy. Heavy
the clasp of fingers. A hard
clutch of weight on my arm.
We move toward the fragrance:
        the pear tree.

The garden lunar. Moonstruck.
Glows. The pear tree clear
in an effulgence of silver
glints. An amphora
of delicate improbable feathers.

Amphora. Nightlamp of
the goddess. Matrona. The Lady.
Maternal deity of dark. The tree
totemic. Sacred. To Hera.
Heraldic as amethyst. Lilac
framed by a height of land:
        northern mountains.

Can I give what I
do not own? Haven
of heaven? Hold out eternal
vellum? Red stitches illumined
        on white linen?

Your tremulous clasp. My
silent assent. We are
Demeter fixed. In search
of bee balm. Focused on
distillations. The mind moves
as the heart. Tidal.

To stand outside. Ex-stasis.
Beyond scythe-time. I cannot
hold the grasp. The raw
necessity of handhold. The unclasping
         of fingers.

We turn in the moon's
pewter path. Retreat
to the stairway. Return
to sewing. Red stitches
parting the white
         of linen.

III

NOCTIS EQUI

Toward dawn
I hear the relentless beat
the thud and thunder
of their hard feet.

They are not slow
these horses of the night.
No impulse from my troubled
sleep murmurs, *lente, lente,*
to those hooves of approaching
                         grief.

They race across
remote terrain morosely
swift violent
nostrils distended
with omens
ill of will.

Frozen in nightmare
I wince nor can I
speak meshed in a terror
as prehistoric as the hulk
of grazing mammoths
who chew on crimes
in the dead light.

In that dead light
the voice of Faustus
shrieks for but one drop
for half a saving drop.

Ovid appears, lunar
Ovid grim in exile
betrayed by fatal fidelity
the need to write consummately
of the erotic itch.

I struggle with disordered
sheets. Catch at the curtains.
Reach for the branch
        of morning.

An open window reaffirms
the absolutes lost to night:

A knowledge of warm
flat rocks facing the sea

green cold water
on a hot day

sunlight after rain
a gull's white wing.

The five simple senses
revived by a fragrant breeze
hear the bird of dawning.
Ordinary daylight suggests
beatitude, the possibles
        of blessedness.

UNRULY WILLS AND AFFECTIONS

I

Brought
into the courtroom
backwards
for fear
her old half-blind
eyes

might confound
chill the abundant
aspects of authority
kill its will
to judge correctly.

They stand before they sit.
Princes and prelates
of the state.
Each
blatant with bias
yet disposed to dispense
Justice.

They are manifold.
Men in folds
of legal parchments
under whose jurisdiction
sheep not women
safely graze.

She is old
fragile but not
infirm.
Accused of witchcraft.

They the gratified
the guardians
of the commonweal
and wealth dare not
risk so much
as a glance
into those burdened
eyes fixed past pain
on powers beyond
pejorative prerogatives.

This is
what is
To Be.
Being:
essence and existence.

When old
and a woman
in the high heyday
of swollen patristic
rage.

To be judged
often
to be condemned
ever.
To be spared
seldom
to be faced
never.
To have few
advocates
and less defence.

Her crime, Satanic:
to cure
with simples
from old wisdom
the sick.

Speak truth
in conundrum.
Tell fortunes
to the unfortunate.

To heal
in a cottage
not in hall
or cell monastic.

Diabolic:
to be old,
female, unattractive
yet have power
to cure, to comfort,
to advise. A paradigm
for death.

Rigid with privilege
rancid with pride
of place and gender
unruly of will
withered of affection,
they warm their eunuch
flesh at her inquisitional
fire.

II

Outside
it is Good Friday
weather.
The heron on the
ragged village shore
fishes at the edge
of dark.
Sorrow sits
on the stiff
arch of his neck.

She walks
in the daze
of a clouded noon
toward the faggots
in the square.

The heron bends
his neck
to fish.

She stumbles
supported by weary
guards not all of them
in love with what
has been commanded.

The town folk watch
some shiver
the prurient
among them
titter.

The sun
sick with disdain
withdraws from the light
the fire gives.

She fixes
her burning ardent
eyes on the sundry
and the multiple
flux
of mortal matter.

Sees her way
through flame
beyond purgatorial
splendour
into the infamy
of men of good
fame
and approved intentions.

She looks.
Her smoke clear
eyes confess
reluctance *to closely
walk* with such
as these to heaven.

THE SHADOW SELF

I reach out
I chant the runes
whisper prayers.
The shadow moves
it will not stay.

The man who comes
for daily bread
refuses wine.

His shadow self
dissolves and fades
will not pause
        at the open gate.

I grasp for hands
touch broken bones.

They sing in my ears
discords of song.

Shadow shadow
on the wall
who's the darkest
one of all?

The sky recedes
the earth retreats
the wind blows chill.

Who knocks at the door?
What knocks at the window pane?

The shadow man
with a pail of crumbs

the shadow man
who will not talk.

Like a dry leaf
in a harsh light

he drops, he drops.

MATRONA LUMINOSA

When I am old
and half asleep drowsing
over old fidelities
I shall move
toward the wisdom
found in the sound
        of water.

Visit in spirit
Parry Falls
where the numinous woman
lives wrapped in a silver net
        of spray
behind walls of falling water.

Driven by outrage
intrepid with anger
embittered she leaves
her people retreats
        into water.

The village shaman
solicitous to repair
injury transforms into a
        striated wasp
flies behind the waterfall
offers conciliation
petitions forgiveness.

Reconciliation accomplished
he leaves.
She remains
a titular deity to
the face of water.

Silence follows
measured by the thaw
of numb arctic devotion.

Above the virtues
of the star-lit heavy
wingèd seraphim descend
as heavenly servants
to mortal manifestation
of the immortal:
the illuminated,
the woman,
Matrona luminosa.

Ancient hierarchies of grace
resonate knowing.
Relate legends of the luminous
the shining woman resplendent
in the concentric circles
           of myth.

Revealing the iridescent
mysteries of pattern
of redemption in the ripples
of moonlight on water
in the voice of the river
a distant view of the sea.

ON PARAGONS, ANIMALS
AND WILD BIRDS

for Patrick Lane

I
Luminous language
can it change
the harsh disorder
   of the real?

Apples on a bough
we wait transparent.
We hope. We feel.
Ask blessings from
   old aching ghosts.

II
   I swim
with cormorants and stately
geese at a rock grey
sea green beach.
Calmed by the scurry
of sandpipers' feet. The
ubiquity of drifting gulls.

   Overhead
the omens fly. Linen
crows call out
the rhythm of a favoured
        verse.

   Warn
of the will to court
the wind. Persephone
gone. Demeter in grief.
The swift disruption
   of the elements.

III
      Rancid men
destroy the goodly beauty
of the world. The poet's mind.
His longing for the perfect
the paragon of animals.
The thirst for virtue
which rewards the fragrance
              of the rose.

IV
      On certain
clear auspicious days
we hear above the noise
persistent rumours.
Echoes of the truth
in which the simple flesh
             delights:
A river flowing through the mist.
Dedicated fish in thick autumnal
             streams.
Evensong on Saints' Days:
        of Ascension
        of Assumption.

V
      In the night sky
triumphantly blue and
dazzling white. Enthroned
in the crescent moon
a radiant child in her arms
the incandescent ikon stands
poised above the delicate
balance of the ebbing tide.

The serpent pressed
beneath her feet
the faltering wind chimes
                signify:

Ritual ceremony and design
are an answer of a partial kind
to blackened cinders. Loss at sea.

IV

THE ALTERED AIR

At the far edge
of the creek I see
the final bloom of summer
in the green salal, the amber
                    of water.

A child sings
where the sand is wet.
Two women read
in the shade of a rowan
                    tree.

Deep in the hectic
red of ripening berries
they sit to read
at peace with mind
                    and matter.

Miraculously free from electronic noise
the nubile young doze
on the hot rocks of late
                    afternoon.

At the quiet end
of evening mist moves
unravelling into the west.

A light breeze
absolves the heat dependent
day's obsession.

Drift-net gulls
their wings turned toward
autumn hover above the transparent
promise of legend.

Perfect harbingers
they offer gifts,
a season of cucumbers
a feast of altered air.

A MANDALA OF BIRDS
AND FEATHERS

The unexpected felicity
of the heron propped
solitary by the irrigation pump.

The white-washed lace of ice
on a waste of wide water.

Black quail nimble
in the frozen orchard.

A mandala of birds and feathers
as visiting finch perch

on the mustard radiance
of a winter willow.

Chill wind, hoar frost
last words spoken

on a walk from southern darkness
into the migratory northern light.

JOSEPH PLASKETT SKETCHING

He stands absorbed
    an abstract in a line
    of trees.
Intent on the lake
    he sketches.

Committed citizen
    of the imagination
    comely as courtesy.
Poised in the politesse of old
            civilizations.
Partial to soft declensions
         slow desuetudes.

Watch as he leans
in the crook of the
        road.
Practised to rescue
the fading afternoon
    from anonymity.

CALLIGRAPHIES OF SILENCE

Species die
as we die
   single in the amber
   warmth of the sun
   sporadic in the pewter
   chill of the moon.

At the last
   driven by a rising wind
   we arrive into the calm
   of welcoming roots.

While stars
stream milk white
   spellbound by distance
   clasped in the luminous
   movement of constellations
Crystal radiances
   cryptic as receding space.

In love with
flight and feathers
   we falter as we move
   in the direction of galaxies
Listen for signals
   missiles
   messengers
Search for
   incandescent umbra
   fading penumbra.

A calligraphy
of silence
   brightens the horizon
   harbours astral accent
   nurtures transcendence.

The music
of delicate bones
    refutes the harm
    in skeletons.

Promises
    singing
    the perfect beauty
    that comes at dark.

BEFORE SLEEP

Rich in heat
the day dissolves
into the black
of last light.

On the terrace
geraniums glow
against darkness.

Birds flutter
talk falls apart.

Starlight scatters
the lucid intervals.

Speech as shadows deepen.

A small breeze
turns the stalks
of wild grasses.

The moon emerges
a round full crystal
hypnotic as light.

AT ENGLISHMAN'S RIVER

for Jim Willer

It is mid-morning
the sun slants on the hot
white outcrop
of opulent rock.

Below
the shallow pool
gives way
enlarges
into the wet green
of dim jade.

A woman
swims
alone in the vivid
bliss of aqueous cold.

Vibrant navigator
she floats
temporary deity
water blessed
blood untrammelled
by the cold
of pebbled river.

A cyclic movement
of limbs
a flex of supple
arm and wrist
stretched to contain
the fluid poise of wild
          water.

V

FESTIVAL HALL, 1955

Thin of ankle
slim of wrist
lithe as riding whips
they teeter on pointed
sartorial slippers correct
in evening dress.

"Frightfully good Mozart
for England, dunt ye think?"

I sit in a corner
of the foyer
beside a clumsy girl
with a score.

She is Russian.
Her glasses are thick.
A companion squints
down his Hasidic
decided nose to peer
at the print.

Across the corridor
a defiant Pole leans
on a rapier thin walking
                stick.

Two elegiac Czechs
gaze toward the stage
for a glimpse of Prague.

Nearby a languid
Slovene asleep
in a nest of tumbled
summer hair leans
away from a hirsute Serb.

53

I ponder on Marx
buried near Hampstead
Heath.

"Frightfully good Mozart,"
he might concur
at a guess
for the politically dispossessed.

HAUTE COUTURE

Watching the ubiquitous
          consumer class
denim-clad darlings of commerce
I ask my sour apple socialist
          heart
Why doesn't the bourgeoisie
          dress bourgeois
          anymore?

Middle aged ladies
in chic shapeless track suits.
Shoes that look designed
          for outer space.
The younger versions in
          grunge
exposed of midriff
navels the cynosure
          of every eye
they hope.

All sheep led blithely
          blind
grazing at the mercantile
          malls of
unaccountable desire.

Once upon a time
farmers wore denim
          overalls or coveralls
and men engaged in hard
          manual labour
          wore denim trousers.
Now it is the fabric
          of academic dress.

Brave new world of violent
                 mercenaries
pedophilic lust
psychotic rage for order
after rape, dismemberment
                 of body parts.

We muse as we settle
                 into atomic dust:
Where and what was
                 the saving, prudent
                 corseted
spatted, bowler-hatted, discreet bourgeoisie?

LIBERATION THEOLOGY
or
A Defence for Islam

I know it is popular
in certain avant-garde circles
to despise Christianity and Judaism
as worn down oppressive creeds
and to turn reverently towards
the scriptures of the East.

Nonetheless, I was startled
to hear at a dinner party
in the southern Okanagan
a worthy woman who spends
time ministering to the destitute
in southern India impervious
to needs on local pavements,
streets or native reserves
because Indian poverty is
exotic and warm
while Canadian poverty is boring
or damp or cold
or all three.

This excellent liberated lady
extolled warmly
the enlightened humanity
of Islam
citing as a case in point
that in contemporary Bangladesh
furious debate raged
over whether two women
who remarried before they
were properly divorced
should or should not
be stoned in some discreet
street or open field.

"Ah ha," I observed,
"Liberation Theology at its best."

Go hang your head,
John Knox, you only harassed
Mary Stuart, one of the privileged
elite, a member of the ruling
class, no less.

Not for you
the moral bravura
of stoning common
ordinary women in Scotland's
dour and sleety streets.

As for that retrograde
prophet, old Jesus,
vigorously objecting to,
not debating, the stoning
of the women taken in adultery,
who was He anyway?
An intolerant fascist nit!
A narrow upstart Jew
disturbing hallowed, time-honoured
                    customs.

Rejoice greatly
veiled women of the Koran
and embattled feminists everywhere.
To stone or not to stone
is now the great doctrinal
schism in parts of Islam.

VI

DOROTHY
or
The Gift

In Memoriam
Dorothy Fraser

Mortal the flesh moves
                 toward silence
mourns as it passes soft
                 voices, voices
                 unattended
which fade into the fragment of dusk
fade at the far edge of hearing.

Born to the sure sound
                 of water
she married in an oasis
brought bloom and blossom
                 to the desert.

Cool recesses resonate
                 in the calm measure
of her hand on the pulse
                 of the keyboard
the grace notes ripple in the vibrance
                 of the aspens
                 the lift of the poplars.

Wolf willow hush at the lakeshore.
Quail scurry in the orchard
as she walks disarming the mist
                 of morning
orioles singing in the branches
                 of her luminous mind.

A gift she had for speaking.
A gift she was from the high gods.

61

Distance she loved and the high
oracular plateaus of healing.
Music she was and brightness
the held breath of seeking
the quest caught in a shaft
                of sunlight.

She lived in the natural hierarchies
                of place
the ripe declivities of southern valleys
the murmur and mutter of rivers
far reaches of lakes clear in
                summer's horizon
in a climate of hot hills gold
                ochred with fruitfulness.

Bring for her memorial
                the flowers of wilderness:
                antelope bush and wild sage
                evening primrose elusive
                Indian paint brush.

A whisper of wind tells us
she who cultivated civil gardens
lingers as essence in the doorway
where she waters a perfumed
armoury of herbs and grasses.

We remember in the silence
the cadence of language
her cadenza of laughter
as shutters open to the night
while a moth flutters in the lamp
                        light.

A gift she was from the high gods.
A book she was of deep dreams.
Now she sings and hums with
          the white stars
the melody of remote radiance
the harmonies of shining
              spheres
                  receding.

DISSOLVING MISTS

In Memoriam
Douglas Plaskett Fraser

                    The sun
is almost directly overhead
the day slips into the patience
                    of afternoon.

A magpie pauses
in the lake poplars. Their leaves
yellow with the end of season
tremble in a small wind.

                    I lean
against the derelict walls
of the decayed Haynes ranch
house. The walls slope
lead into the weathered shade
                    of memory.

Once
home for cattle fattening
in the summer meadows
they stand apart
meshed in slow erosions
worn guardians fatal
sentinels of time revealed.

                    The day
like the year begins
to decline into mute
                    brilliance.

He left on such a day. A day
in high autumn, late summer.
Left the dry orchards resonant
                    of old deserts.

64

Walked away
from the scent of sage
the petal of blossom reward
of ripened fruit.

Beyond the river
a marsh hawk dips
and rises. Deliberate
poised to strike.

                    I recall
his hand raised. Binoculars
held to an eye trained
to discern species observe
                    identity in flight.

Our friend
sketches against the immutable
hills. Arresting the flux
of movement. Fixed on transcendence
he makes matter translucent.

The flawless afternoon
gathers for completion.
Calm as the river eddy
unfastening, flowing toward us.

              The hush
of his voice hovers
over the water. The quiet
of lips parted to say
farewell to speech forever.
              Yet
leaving behind syllables
articulations in the murmur
of water among rocks.

Lost to us.
At home with the far
winds, the late star. We
remember as he left,
the perfection of knowing
summer before the dissolving
                mists of autumn.

A BITTERN IN THE SNOW

In Memoriam
Alvin Balkind

Light falls where it may
darkness comes unbidden
and Time lies like a cobweb
                    in the mind.

Yesterday, I walked through
                    unaccustomed snow
watching for tomorrow.

The landscape aptly named
                    Terra Nova
tells of loss, lies flat
as final goodbye
blessed by the orange swoop
of the marsh hawk's flight.

There is snow and silence.

A peremptory shift in the wind
parts the reedy sedge
below the dyke
where sentient still
the bittern stands
                    stone stark.

A movement of the neck
and I am lost
in the enigmatic glitter
of its bird-bright eye.

It signals winter
speaks of absence
departure over deep untroubled
          water
replies farewell
to God be with you.

Reminds the heart
the last frost of evening
reveals frozen beauty
a memory of leaves falling
praise for the pure art
          of being.

VII

THE TASTE OF SILENCE

It arrives
unannounced
savoured between
the toss and touch
      of the sea
on sharp pebbled
      sand.

I think back
on an evening
      of music.
Watch the cellist
with the face of a
      young hawk
caught in the meditative
      poise of flight.

His arm a wing
of grace notes
sweeps the circumference
      of radiance
the radicals of treble.

Outside
in grey mist
the delicate hemlock
      bough bends.

The cellist
intent on his strings
black sleeved
black browed
bows against
      the light.

In the museum
totemic faces
emerge sculptural
patterned against
the pewter dusk.

They listen
permissive as patience.

In the aftermath
of intermission
in the affinities
of interlude
the pianist
perfect accomplice
luminous accompanist
touches the incandescences
of her instrument
the cellist his strings.

Each weaves
a caress of dialogue
stroking the ear
with fingers of silk
codes of complicity
beyond time and blemish.

The dying fall
that tastes of silence.

THE LUMINOSITY OF FROST

Late September. River
water stains the ocean
amber. Elemental blue
and green transmute into
                    the serene of autumn.

In the shallows. By
the capacious rock five
mergansers dip and dive
into a froth of saline tea.

Distant but audible. A man
cries out. Sick with rage
at the fire within. Infirmity
without. Where he lives
                    is always North.

The tide floods in. In full
aquatic bliss insouciantly glad
the mergansers swim. Grace
and favour in their webbed
insistent limbs they dart. Against
                    the flux of light
they capture ordinary sight.

Real as today. Apparent
yet apart from the length
of shade gathered below
the conifer crowded trees
on the west shore. They bob
                    and float.

I move past. In retreat
from tidal cold. Reach
towards a shore bathed
in the last of yesterday.

The eye bemused by water. Looks
for stones. Anticipates the cool
luminosity of frost. How it
tempts towards a width
                of white to patience.
Hope in arduous breath.
The far scope of distance.
Plenitude. The felicities
                of flight.

STAINS OF THE ETERNAL

Watching him rescue the fading
afternoon from anonymity, I contemplate
his larger issues: fireplaces with
Venetian mirrors, summer tables
and winter repasts.

Reflections on what we live
with and what we leave behind
paramount as memorabilia. Insubstantial
pageants made substantial. Coloured
shadows given substance. Bridges
built to walk toward *temps*
perdu.

The poetics of windows, their politic
lens of perception richer than
summer followed by apple harvest
on the simplicity of round tables.

Triumphant illusion discarded for the
reality of vibrant life crowds
the canvas. Islands of felicity
caught in webs of filtered light.

The meditative pose of hollyhocks
in a Suffolk garden. They touch
the heart with mortal longing.
Cleopatra crowned and sceptred,
immortality defying oblivion.

Everywhere the stains of the
eternal seep into corners. The
radiant fire aslant the musing
girl pensive in repose.

Duration, existence sublimated
into a dream of doorways. Exits
and entrances. The tranced
coming and going. Cathedral bells
distanced. Echo of marble marvels.

Totemic fingers point toward
a darkening height. The dark
that follows where we cannot
go caparisoned in chandeliers.

Lucid ambition blending the
present with ease into the
reportage of the past. The pain
and pleasure of a species
aspires to achieve the ineffables
                    of music.

Celestial the harmonies some
say in nature, some in art. We
find *le mot juste* in each.
The desire for the incandescent
transcendence of the rose.

Movement points to stillness.
A fragrance of flowers distilled
into a witness for angels—
focused on the milk white
core of a lifted brush we
love with love of the recording
                    partial eye.

CIRCLES AND PAINTED HORSES

In Memoriam
Ralph Gustafson

> *... The painted horse*
> *goes into that darkness where all circles go.*
> Patrick Lane

The painted horse. Darkness.
I write of concentric circles
turning into light. Summer
grief turns those circles dark.

My circles spin. A vatic silence
speaks to the poet of the carousel.
He draws those sinuous charts
of darkness where all circles
go. His painted horse faithful
as the sun returning after rain
emerges grave with augury.

In childhood
I loved cold. Longed for
the inviolates of snow. Evening
ultimates of violet light. Now
late and large in life I know
the harder core of ice.

Old friends
clear in the heart and dear
as the bells of morning climb
the painted horses. Ride soft
eyed into galactic distance.

77

Leave me to gaze
at mullioned windows. Lookouts
of memory. Framed by the lattice
of time shared. Windows lit
by the flicker of a heart bright
with the patina of farewell.

Slow horse. Fading
anchored rider. Reins restive with
longing for pattern. Design to defeat
depredation. Respond to the silver
of water. The firm earth of healing.
Green gratitude in the arms of sleep.

ABOUT THE AUTHOR

Marya Fiamengo is one of Canada's truly fine women poets. For nearly four decades now, she has been publishing work of unusual distinctiveness. Intelligent, richly evocative, formidable in its clarity, lyrical and yet scrupulous, passionate and yet austere, the voice in Fiamengo's poems is like no other in Canadian poetry.

From the beginning of her literary career, Fiamengo's central imaginative preoccupation has been history. Her cultural inheritance as the British Columbia born daughter of Yugoslavian immigrants has taught her an attentiveness to history that is acute; it has also intensified her unabashed nationalism as a Canadian, and her awareness of Canadian history, culture, and landscape.

While Fiamengo has acknowledged the forces of history, she has also deeply explored the ways in which the pressures of history are registered in individual lives. In addition to being a Canadian nationalist, she is a socialist and what she herself has termed a "moderate feminist." Fiamengo has, in fact, contributed to Canadian poetry some of its best, most irrefutably powerful feminist poems. On the one hand, these poems focus on the struggle on the part of women for legitimate power; on the other, they address the paradox that women have innate power. The voice in these works is that of the strong female—passionate, self-possessed, ironic, intellectually honed, dauntless.

In *White Linen Remembered*, Fiamengo's concern for the vitality of the individual often lends her poems an expressly elegiac tone. In turn, the writing here expands on the theme of the power of art to heal and console the inevitables of human loss. The poet can now be understood as one who has looked at once to the external—to the events and movements within history—and to the internal—to the everlasting present of the most meaningful events within the human psyche, meditating on the origins of personal identity, and ultimately on the imponderables of the divine. The voice is noteworthy for its wisdom, colour, and grace.

Poems from Fiamengo's seven books have appeared in several anthologies, among them *40 Women Poets, The Penguin Book of Canadian Verse,* and *Sealed in Struggle: Canadian Poetry and the Spanish Civil War,* where her "Acknowledge Him Canadian" is both her tribute to Norman Bethune and a celebration of the spirit which informs Canadian identity. Recent work by Fiamengo has been anthologized in *Words We Call Home* and *Inside the Poem.*

Brought up and educated in B.C., Marya Fiamengo taught Canadian literature for many years at the University of British Columbia. She is now retired and lives in West Vancouver.